It Would Be Wise Not To Ask For Lemons

Poems by Simone Le Ann

This Book Is A Bomb!
www.ThisBookIsABomb.com

Book design by Jonathan Lee Byrd

ISBN 978-0-9830364-2-5
Library of Congress Control Number 2011931029

Printed in the United States of America

Я тоскую без Вас

The Word of the Day Is Brindled

I question my existence,
I question my "Faith?"
I accuse my heart,
Because it easily breaks,
I question my memories,
I question my past,
I can't see a future,
The good never does last,
I question my death,
I question my life,
Will there ever be more?
Are these questions a cure?
The cure of faith,
The cure of thought,
The strength of Love,
Even if,
It was all a lost cause,
We are given,
The chance to pause,
Breathe in,
Exhale,

Exhausted . . .

The eternal rest.

Paranoid Insomniac

Is it the paranoia or the pills?
Either way, I've got my fill,
Not on fuel and not on sleep,
But on secrets, I secretly keep,
Keeping time is no concern,
Lost the concept, lost my turn,
Losing weight and gaining bone,
Loner wolf is all alone,
I can't hold on to a moment,
As miniscule as sand,
Slips through translucent skin,
And burns into my hand,
Seeping into blood stream,
The clots continue to grow,
Inching higher every moment,
Down, Down,
Further I go.

Cinco de fucked up

Cheers to what's been said,

Cheers to what's been done,

Cheers to what it was,

I assure you, it was fun,

I am alive and living,

You're a song I was singing,

In the shower,

So I couldn't be heard.

Hangover or bad memory?

I bit off more then I could chew,
Swallowed the whole thing whole,
Now I'm choking . . . what's new?
I've poured too much milk,
Into my cereal bowl,
Put my boots on, strapped on tight,
Who knows where my change will take me tonight,
I've met a thousand faces,
I've thanked a thousand more,
I walked a hundred traces,
Slept on a hundred floors,
If I were asked to rewind and look back,
I'd say "I'm not sure what to see",
My memory is a boarded up house...no cracks,
I don't recall who I used to be,
If you gave me a mirror and said "smile",
I'd make a face and frown,
Not able to fake it, even for awhile,
I'd rather rub my feet and stare at the ground,
You gave me a dollar, said "play a song",
You smirked at the jukebox,
If I liked you, I'd be set,

But the timing is wrong,

And I do not like you...

One bit.

I'm sorry it's your birthday

For whoever finds this,
I've been lost too long,
Wake, brush teeth, pills, work,
Home, get wasted, pass out,
Wake, comb hair, pills, brush teeth,
Swish, spit, smile, repeat,
It's the next day, same deal,
Gimme the bottles, This is how to feel,
My teeth grind to rot out,
My skin is peeling new,
My heart sinks with doubt,
My brain has got a stomach flu,
My bones shake and grind,
Steady myself, smile, I'm fine,
To whoever does find me,
I just need you to know,
365 Nails in my coffin,
But my nails never grow,
If you call before noon,
I'll still be asleep,
You want to see me soon?
Well . . . just make it brief.

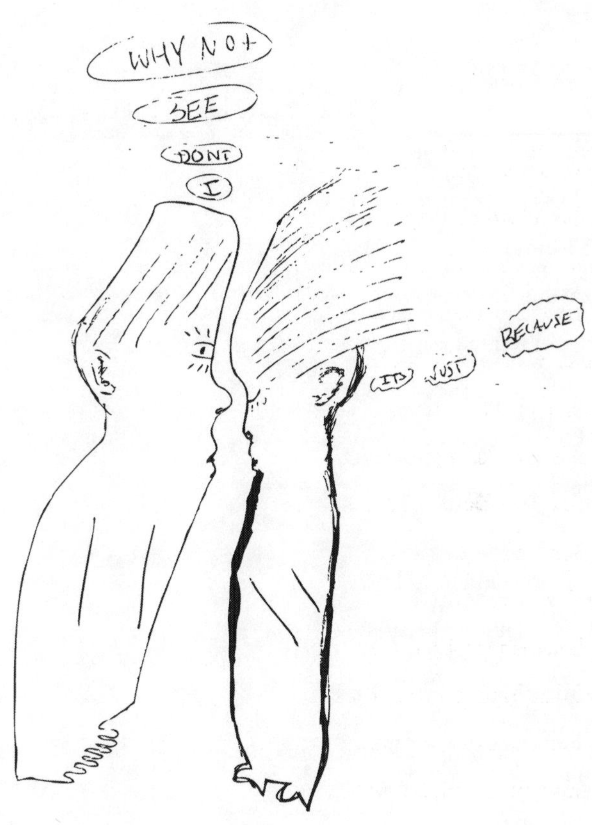
WHY NOT
SEE
DONT
I
ITS
JUST
BECAUSE

I got roots in my boots

His hand is not what I choose,
His lips are kissing me,
The hands been chosen,
The words then spoken,
And all I wanted was your city bed,
Your shaking hands,
And fucked up head,
I could have the world,
But I just want your town,
My name could be in lights,
But you wouldn't be around,
So now down to the bottom line,
Do I sink or Swim?
Or just ride along,
For you to tug and toss,
This is your loss,
It's a new year,
I'm a new soul,
Pulling out my roots,
I'll find new ground,
Plant myself and grow,
Grow up buttercup,

Your love is a show,

I despise old episodes.

She's actually 92

We took the elevator,
Stood at your bedside,
Waited for movement,
For your eyelids to rise,
You spoke anyway,
"I can't, I won't do that."
You said you spoke with the devil,
We want to save you,
After so long, nothing we can do,
So, we stand at your feet,
Fight the demons with you,
To stay safe and brave,
Maybe it's the medication,
Or just old age,
Either way, we are here,
Keep you out of that cage,
Please don't get up again,
Every time you fall, weakness gives in,
Be strong Elva,
Be strong,
We'll stay by your bedside,
You've done nothing wrong.

365 = 5 times 4 - 1

Its not easy . . . no,

When you're caught in undertow,

Do not swim against it,

Only further in you'll go,

Until you lose sight,

Of what you used to know,

You have to except change,

If not, you will decay,

It's tough to re-arrange,

A calendar full, of yesterday.

Story Time

Gather 'round children,
It's a story short of smile,
But it's a lesson we all learn,
Some just wait a while,
Longer.

You'll remember this one,
Once I near the end,
If you start to feel lonely,
Sit close to a friend,
To keep you company.

They shuffle and greet,
They sit, cross feet,
Now this story,
Is one you won't forget,
Full of empty love & lies,
Memories of pure regret.

I go on and on,
Story becomes song,
So I sing, and cry,
The children,

Don't understand why,
I'm crying harder.

They say "why",
"Why do you tell this story?"
I say for the truth,
It is glue that holds us,
It is truth that molds us,
They point upward and say,
"But he",
"He will hold you",
"He will dry your eyes",
I laugh.

I say my dear children,
Someday you will see,
Through your parents lies,
Eyes open, eyes dry,
I pat my back,
Metaphorically.

The children smile,
I say,
This is not a happy story,

This is life,
You're born,
You live,
You die.

They say,
"We know",
"But it's okay",
"Because like you said",
"Life is a lie".

Springing forward, still Falling behind

Change your mind,

Adjust the time,

Can't re-wind,

So on we march,

It's now April,

We can always look back,

Don't stare too hard,

You'll break your own heart.

Four season reasoning

In the buds of spring,
You wonder what she'll bring,
Maybe hope, maybe cure,
Maybe a deep sleep,
Comfortable and pure.
Like the mute mouth baby,
Clinging to mother,
You hope for that change,
For the grace of summer,
It comes and goes,
Just as the rains and snows,
You'd like something to stick,
Weather changes make me sick.
You've got to live for the day,
And that's not just to say,
Do not live for tomorrow,
But we are NOT promised one,
Bask in the sun, Break in the shade,
Meet me in the stream,
There we can wait and wade,
For tomorrow,
We can only dream.

Adam and Eve
Ate only once

I've been fighting for your eyes, since 1989,
Been searching for your soul,
Since I thought I found mine,
Couldn't catch a break, Couldn't catch my fall,
You made a big mistake,
That night you didn't call,
I kept my fingers laced,
I kept my eyes on you,
Watched, as you traced,
The lines we walked,
Two by Two,
You promised you'd show,
Glued myself to the clock,
Watched the hours slowly go,
Never saw you turn the block,
Coming into reason,
Made up a new season,
Name given is "let down",
Cause I know you won't be around,
And if by chance you do return,
Your dresser will still be packed,

Broken promises are a subject to learn,

Left by leaves,

Staying alive,

Let down season is three sixty-five.

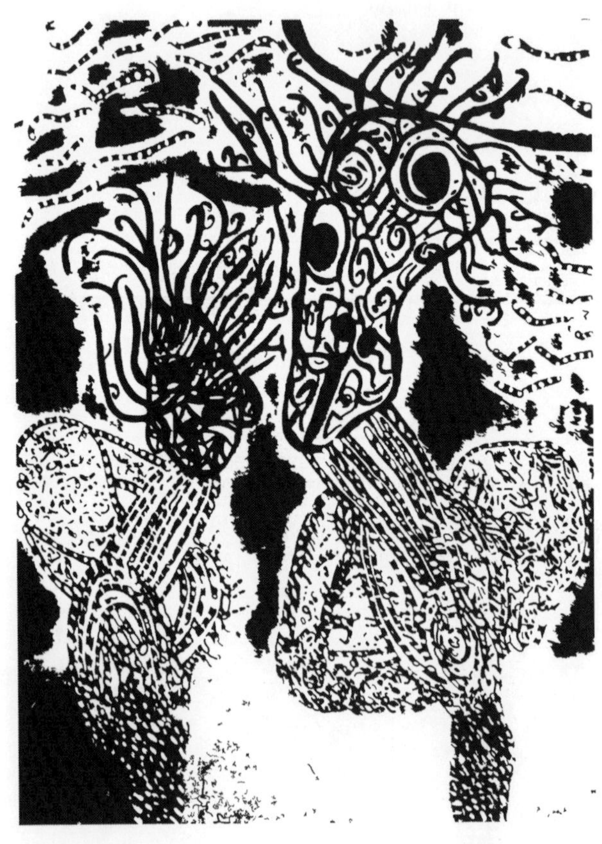

Tis-used

I'm your handkerchief,
You're "just in case",
The crumbling flowers,
In a water-less vase,
The pedals fall, too brittle to press,
I threw them out, then got dressed,
The new day starts, I stretch and wake,
Put myself together, Smile at the mirror,
Even though it's fake,
You may enter my life,
We will laugh and you will love,
You try to hold my hand,
But I don't need another glove,
I hardly exist, I don't believe,
I am always on the run,
But never really leave.

Full from taxi cabs

Don't know where to put my hands,
Next to clean cookie cutting businessmen,
You baked another dozen,
My fingers are too frozen to eat,
What you want is not what you need,
Its all summer vs.: winter,
If you call tonight, I won't be around,
Probably drunk downtown,
Spending my money on cab fair,
Nothing is fair,
Nothing is ending,
We will just keep pretending,
That summer is around the corner,
Pass it along.

Algebraic Expression

We spoke about this; you never said a word,

I said it all,

I gave advice and a high five,

You gave me your two cents and a free ride,

Your word went out the window,

Became a memory,

I wished to keep it,

Disappointed,

Cannot retrieve it,

You gave me a pat on the back,

Now, on you go,

To another smile,

To another show,

Well . . . I love you if it counts,

You're no good with math.

Vodka is cheaper than Fast Food

We've found comfort in the past,

Yet we stay glued to the calendar, And to fate,

The liquor burns, at an alarming rate,

I pass the pleasure,

I pass the time,

Instead of a nickel, She gave me a dime,

I looked up and smiled,

"Thank you",

"This will be just fine."

Riding Waves

Catching colds,
Getting old,
Our stories collect dust,
We're left to rust or rot,
Picked through, and picked apart,
They'll tear out your insides,
Leave you ashamed and crying,
I guess this is dying.
Shifting lanes, pulled ahead,
Congrats Comrade,
We fought against the current,
Catch a wave,
We deserve it,
Instead we caught a tidal wave,
Wave goodbye,
See you in the rip tide.

Libra's Downfall

The months swim by,
Caught in the current,
When will I learn it?
I've become your crutch,
Your helping hand,
Your sleeping lush,
Your foot in the sand,
I placed the holy bible,
On my coffee table,
For my guests to feel at ease,
I simply aim to please.

Treating a Trick

You are my sunshine,
My only sunshine,
And so it hurts me to say,
The future I see,
Includes you everyday,
I know you don't want that,
Neither do I,
But it's the feelings inside,
That just won't die,
I'd give you your medicine,
But you'll just hide it under your tongue,
Wait 'til I walk away,
Then throw it out,
To yesterday.

Vaccine

If you ever claim ill,
I will be by your side,
Fetching tissues,
Pulling over the ride,
We'll ride it out together,
I'll grab your sweater,
A prescription can cure you,
Love is a virtue,
I promise to stay,
No matter the time it takes,
For you to get well,
You can count my love,
I will count the coughs,
When the number gets low,
You won't think of me at all,
It's fact and I know it,
But still I stay,
Make the lonely,
Go away.

Tornado Watch

Down my neck,
Down my spine,
Drown me out,
In a bottle of wine,
Wasting ink,
Wasting time,
Waste is slimmer,
When all you have is a dime,
Ten pounds gone,
We'll see how far this goes,
Until I can't feel my toes,
My body aches in sleep,
Alarm goes off,
And my limbs remain numb,
So little one can do,
When they can't feel their thumbs.

Roundtrip City

If only it were possible to live in memories,
Then I'd be content,
I'd rather live in the past,
Than to have a future,
Is this so wrong of me?
I'd like to remove my eyes,
Wash them in bleach,
Shake them dry, Replace,
I've seen nothing new the past few years,
It's time for a change.
I am better off a vegetable,
Alive and breathing,
But holds no feeling,
This is who I am really,
Just without hospital bracelet

My newest fail

I thought this a lark,
My simple Noah's ark,
Guess I should have known,
All those daydreams,
Are still homegrown,
I surrender at lion's den,
To the never again,
This is no laughing matter,
When it rains... It pours,
I'd rather stay indoors anyway,
I'm choosing you,
Please return the favor,
Its lost all flavor,
Melted ice cream,
I lost my voice.

Poor Man's Diet

Lethargic and nostalgic,
Well, they go hand in hand,
One silver, one gold,
But no one's cashing in,
Time is money honey,
This five-dollar bill,
Won't get me very far,
Driving to work,
Home, Back to work,
But sleeping in your car,
Bring a pillow and blanket,
Something to keep you warm,
I will bring the laughter,
And comfort from the storm,
All I ever wanted was short story time,
But you flashed those bedroom eyes,
Sure, I said okay,
Not what I meant to say,
I meant to grab my shoes,
Strap 'em on and hit the road,
Too bad I left them in the backseat,
Like the way you think of me.

Mornin' September

Time isn't moving,
The sun just won't set,
All a gambled hand,
I dare make a bet,
Chips tossed in,
I hit the rim,
Bounced back,
Back to bed,
Head for the hills,
The ambulance is lost.

Steel-toed Boots

Take a walk in my shoes,
Tell me your ankles don't bruise,
Wearing out the soles,
Wandering the streets,
Parking lot full, I feel nothing,
For those I meet,
Laying in your bed,
Hand in Hand, Head to chest,
I watch your lungs, Fill and rest.
Just leave before two,
I feel nothing for you.

Can’t seem to Get too far

She's got her Walkman and whiskey,
You leave a voicemail "come kiss me",
You shrug and smile,
Make her wait a while,
She calls a cab; you call it a night,
She buckles up; you turn off the light,
You wrap up in covers,
With your newest lover,
For now anyway.
She arrives at your door,
Pitter, Patter,
Pity on the floor,
Shoving her back into the black,
You don't even attempt to look back.
Cuddle up, cuddle monster.

Autumn Breeze

Five years past,
Nothing will last,
They say, "Never say never",
But what's holding you together?
Is it the stitch or the crutch?
Who's hand will you hold?
I sold my luck,
In tins and soda cans,
Give me strength,
To begin again,
Forget those days,
Forget that mouth,
Hide under blankets,
And go down south.

I’m sorry

I'd almost rather be boxed in,
Than free to fuck up,
I've found four leaf clovers,
But I'm still fucking you over.

Sleeping in

It’s a milestone,
Then lost and forgotten,
The big bang,
The big break,
Don't drink the water,
Drink the whiskey,
Call me silent,
Call me tomorrow,
I find it funny,
You're going to call at all,
You use me,
I don't mind it,
I'd fight it, but I like it,
My bed still holds your bones,
In my closet still hang your clothes,
My heart still holds the memories,
But I have no hand to hold.

Thread and Stitch

It's a needle on a record,

It's a hand on a clock,

Weighing me down,

Ticking to the tock,

Right hand,

Left Hand,

Don't hand me off.

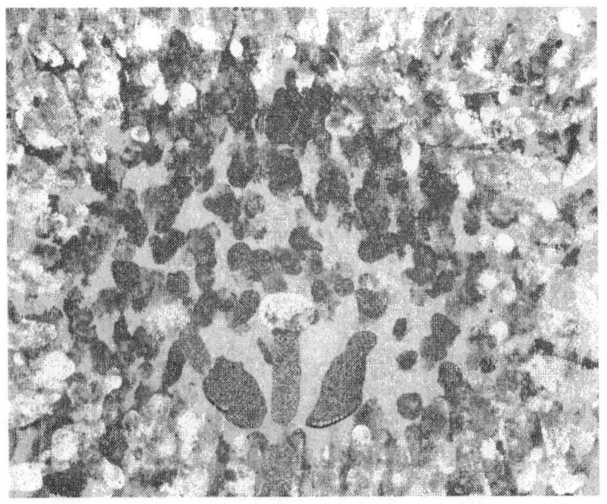

Finger prick

Robots in 3 by 4's,
Checking our wrists,
Watching the doors,
Four hours of sleep,
Still fucking awake,
Stuck in zombie state.
Eyes yellow and glazed,
Liver severed, lungs in rage,
Weak knees for the weekends,
You're the cure for Monday blues.
In every drag, I drag behind my bricks,
Making my spine twist, and my stomach sick.
Keeping track of the letters, Please get better,
Soon.

Western

Lets settle this tonight cowboy,
You can walk down that dusty old road,
And call that rabbit hole your home,
You cover up with dirt and shame,
Only God knows you'll never be the same.
These drought filled days have killed you,
And on and on, that fox will claim your body,
Point north and taste the breeze,
Wind whispers how you're bound to freeze,
Keep on running, in circles, in time, in and out,
Breathe.
You'll find tumbleweed motionless,
And kick around the rock less landscape,
Find the Valley that sucked you in,
A tunnel, enclosed, bright-lit city,
You are hallucinating tonight.
So close to gone but still standing,
The sky is offering rest,
Take this chance,
Take this win,
Lightening has struck so close to home,
And a fox like you can sense it,
Trip your staggered sway this way,

Left or right?

Arrows become your mind,

Scarecrow has chosen my lifeline.

Dusty lanes, and howling lies,

The sky asleep, so rest your eyes.

Sleep under the nothing cowboy.

Trapped in a Haunted House

A life that's become dependent on waiting,

But time never sits well with me,

It sits and stews,

Like the mornings and afternoons,

I wasted time with you.

Complete with sash and wave,

The attention you crave,

Forever in denial,

You love to hate yourself.

I've never seen eyes so empty,

Until I found myself trapped in a Haunted House.

Flight 714

I'm leaving this cardboard town,
Goin' down south,
Yeah I'm goin' down,
Can't really feel my legs,
And my chest is pretty heavy,
Weighing me down,
Yeah I'm going down,
Watch my plane take off,
If I crash . . . I crash.
The houses are growing,
We're goin' back down,
Back to cardboard town.
My watch was broken.
But time kept going,
So I threw it out,
Yeah, threw it down,
Home sweet home . . . Cardboard town.

Left footed

If in the morning,
I do wake,
I hope my life,
Was no mistake?
And if by night,
I toss and turn,
I hope someday,
You will return.
Bedside, right side, fast asleep,
I'll keep you safe in my pocket,
Or tightly tucked in my locket,
The hand that feeds is the one you hold,
No one by my right side,
This is getting old.

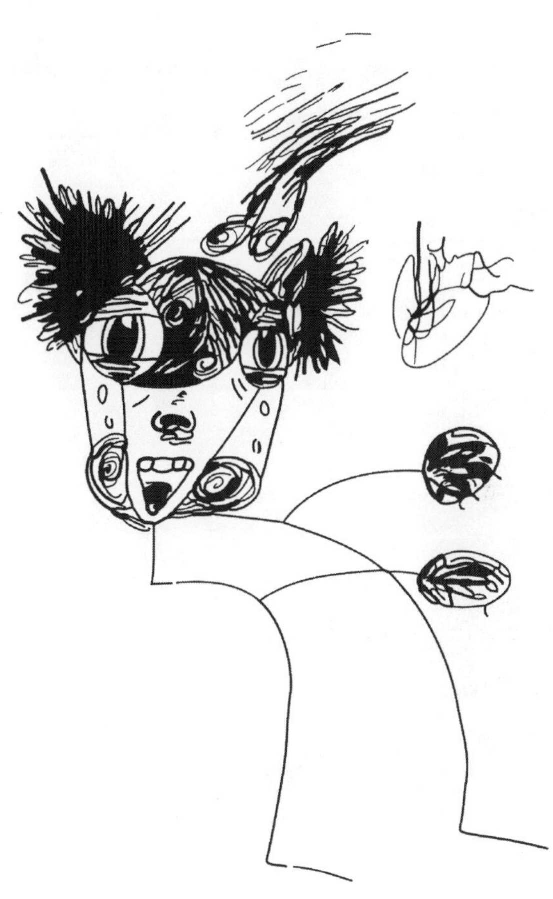

It was storming November 5th

It's the thought of what was,
That's always crossing my mind,
Hold in my breath,
Crossing over my eyes,
Almost over the bridge,
Almost but not quite.
Cast a reel, got a bite,
The bridge caught fire,
Between love and liar,
Could be and was,
What not and because.
And in the chill of September,
I only remember November.

Bucket Lust

You threw me away like an old pair of shoes,
Changed the channel like some bad news,
Thoughtless ideas,
Meaningless conversations,
A dull sign in a dull town,
Welcome to my life.

Buckle up for safety, Please

Seat by seat,
Foot by feet,
Hand in hand,
Heart inside,
Wrapped up in coffee cups,
A carton or 2 just because,
You can count on me to meet you,
Just don't expect me to be on time,
We can sit against this wall,
I'm not promising a free fall.

Meet me in Savannah

When your heart is too big,
And you can't love yourself,
You project that love,
Onto somebody else,
I dipped my hand in boiling honey,
Reached out an arm for someone to find me,
A bee flew in but we just didn't click,
He lasted 20 minutes, my heart still sick.
I've got another plan, a morbid excuse,
To hang my head, become a recluse,
When I was given the 10 digits,
I couldn't resist,
Car ride, to park side,
The most humble of bees,
Made me weak at my knees.
As the honey thickens and dries,
You kept it clean, Shooed away the flies,
I know you're known to sting,
But I will keep busy as a bee,
Awaiting my phone to ring.

5 days & 50 bucks

The 5'o clock kept me alive,
Staying sane between white lines,
Everyone boxed in his or her own lives,
Body shakes as leaves,
Limbs steady tree trunks,
I don't mind the dark tonight,
You are by my side,
You gave me two shoulders and a leg up,
I gave my time and half empty cup,
Let's call it a night,
Forgetting who we are,
I died in my bones,
Born again in your car.

Pencil Pusher

The image of you,
Imbedded in my head,
Of your naked body,
Stretched in her bed,
You're no different,
Matter of fact,
You're worse,
Doomed from the start,
A platonic curse,
Mercy me,
Show me just how,
This battle is won,
With plague and sin,
Did we begin?
Take my word,
Or throw me on trial for survival.

Vacuum town
Sucking you down

If you plead and beg,
She'll never feed you,
Patiently patient,
Legs dangling from chair,
Hands high in the air,
Screaming, No one's there,
No, no one cares.
All I am left with,
Is an empty wallet?
With taste buds for copper,
I've got this coffee mug,
Should settle my nerves,
But my stomach churns,
Watch the butter form,
Foam on top,
Blow off some steam.

Arrhythmia Love

All those bulletproof vests,
Just don't stand a chance,
In a world of win or loose,
Heads or tails of lies,
Flip a coin of "fate",
A 50-50 chance,
Hold in your breath,
Watch it hit the ground,
Eyes of black holes,
Closest to heart break.
Arrhythmia Love keeps this heart beating,
Burberry perfume to cover up smoke,
Breathing in deep, and sharp,
Razor blades to the throat,
Cold air, hitting hard,
When you take those steps,
The first steps to disaster,
Stumble down another mile,
Tripping off broken words you can't even pronounce.
What a life to lead in the wrong direction.

Dead silence
Does not kill

I hope for your voice,
But hopeless I remain,
Consumed in routine,
I am not ashamed,
Who's to blame?
The air is smooth,
The warmth can kill,
Rain clouds swarm,
I've lost my sunshine,
To this dead silent night.

Face down the Gutter side

Kiss me once for good luck,
Kiss me twice and it's deadly,
Kiss me for a third, heavenly,
Dirty trash filled land in time,
When will you ever be mine?
A week is far too long,
Two weeks will kill me,
It's only been a day,
And I miss you already.
Stitch a broken heart,
Words cannot replace,
I will meet you on the platform Friday,
I don't care how long the wait,
I just need your face.

Hand together

So you hide your regret,

In the back of your head, But I can see it.

When you look in my eyes,

And I guess I'm just waiting,

For the truth and all the answers,

But maybe I'm asking the wrong question.

How ashamed you must feel,

How dead you must see yourself,

Can you even be honest with your heart?

So afraid to live and love,

So, fear came crawling inside,

And you slipped through her doorway,

With every foul intention,

I don't want this anymore,

I'm ready to move on with my life,

3 years wasted on a 3-month fuck,

The future isn't looking so bright,

If I would have known sooner,

I wouldn't have held you back so long.

Go fly home now bird,

I can only hope you'll hit the ground,

Then maybe I will have the guts to ask,

If it is only comfort dear,

I don't want to be around.

Not today, not tonight,

The question I asked . . .

Well, you answered it just right.

Ocean Shitty Is number 9

If the night nears black,
I won't look back,
The sun is rising on the East side,
And we're going out west,
Back home to rest,
Conquer my quest,
Found a car,
Slept inside,
No blankets around,
Just came for the ride,
A dollar twenty five,
But I will be just fine,
Default, My fault,
Turning in revolt,
Attach, Detach,
Sew another scheme.

Tuxedos and Cheap Wine

His words like a dirge,
Audience smiling at a funeral,
Men in matching black attire,
Funeral takes the role play,
Actors have taken their vacations,
No one, with no one thing to say,
They simply acknowledge their existence,
Wave you off into the distance.

You had me At Goodbye

He polishes his trophy,
To make momma proud,
But she doesn't care,
Never has.
Spends an hour on one scratch,
And removing the dust,
So much time wasted,
When he should have just given up.
When your arms sway,
On a sleepless Saturday,
I'll just stay home again,
Momma, please don't come in.
You left me at hello,
And had me at Goodbye,
Church bells are ringing,
Forgiveness in session,
Confessional booth: a waiting line,
Take a number from the wall,
Wait to be called,
Forgetting what you had to confess.

I WAS
MISLEA

Coke used to Be cheap

Straying from becoming persistent,
I simply admire from a distance,
Never to fall distant,
For you are the only one to listen,
Now I'm feeling senseless,
Losing all direction,
A cris-cross pattern,
Leaves me feeling dizzy,
And forever thoughts are messy,
Messing with my mind,
Always losing track of time,
Seems I can never really find,
Any sort of change in this place,
A penny, a nickel, not even a dime,
Fearful of falling into line,
And no one by side,
To pick me up on this ride,
Driving to no return,
Striving for a note to burn,
A chorus line falls flat,
Tripped and fell on my face,
Testing motionless on the floor,

Cluttered thoughts,

Expecting more,

Never the less . . . I'll keep searching.

Morning Piss

When the tide rose high,
You cursed the sky,
The ship thrashed and fell,
And you cursed yourself,
But they all wished you well,
Then the sun rejoined the clouds,
And you cursed the one in charge,
He promised eternity, he promised life,
So you spat at his faith as well as his wife,
You've never been able to go out on your own,
And knowing you at all, they shouldn't leave you alone,
You'll scratch and pick, til it makes you sick,
This time you've cursed your claws,
With every creature that spoke in your dreams,
Their eyes so bright, their words pristine,
When the day arrived,
You've awoken from thought,
And were able to mumble "happiness can't be bought",
Once the day comes, you lay your demons to rest,
That's when he loved you most, and saw you at best.

Manic Depressed

When the flood rushed in and all hope was lost,
Your mind was blocked, and you wished death at any cost,
So your fingers danced on the silver buttons, trembling,
Yet a beat was kept, and that's when you met me,
Not one of us spoke, but the silence was loud,
We walked in, one, by two and you cried "You make me proud,"
So, there, the grin accompanied with a river,
My body so numb, my brain held the shiver,
The switch, the strap, the last look back,
Once inside fastened tight, a smirk was cracked,
"There she is," . . . "Knew you could smile",
"I'm just scarred sir.", then met white walls and tile,
My hefty head hung like a screw not securely in place,
Body, a broken board, and joined by pale face,
Hours passed on highways, no news, no hope,
But in session I explained inside "we all need to cope,"
Last call of the night, in awe of what was said,
Maybe I do have a plan, for once I'm glad I'm not dead.

GUESS
I
AM
STILL
HERE...
STRANGE

Election day

The farmers won't grow,
The public won't pay,
We're feeding off frenzy,
And love for dismay,
Disassemble the campaign,
Break down every line, every lie,
No bread on the table,
But four mouths to feed,
Bite into the ice,
Chip off the block.

Weary week

The days make me weak,
But the weeks make me strong,
I know I must speak,
But the timing is so wrong,
Oh gracious one,
I thank you for your honesty,
Seldom have I smiled alive,
Oh cowardless wind,
Blow across my shoulders,
Love is no game or toy,
More of a false statement said far too much,
I love you not,
Forget me now,
A good 3 cheers,
To a wasted 3 and a half years,
One, two, three, four,
What's the point in counting anymore?

We own the night, we own the woods

You are the wolf,
I am the fox,
I must be brave,
I must be brave,
I've faced a million suns,
And circled a million moons,
When I wasn't as strong,
But now, I must be brave,
I drank from the lake,
Waited in the stream,
Tonight my enemy may claim me,
But I must be brave,
My den collapsed,
Pups inside,
Every tear I faced head on,
I must be brave,
I wish my home back,
I wish my pups alive,
But tonight I wish for bravery,
I must be brave,
I must be brave.

December had me

My bones are itching for hooded walks with you,
Maybe grab a coffee or two,
I'll learn to shut my mouth,
If you can keep it closed,
I'm sick of walking in circles around you so clothed,
Undress my innocence, in the premature winter cold,
I'm pitching out the cores from the fruit you decided to eat,
I've bought a dozen apples, each one rotten,
Do I regret the breaking of clouds?
Or finding your face in crowds?
Walking on dirty carpet floors never felt much like home,
But the bottle count brings me comfort, I'm not alone.

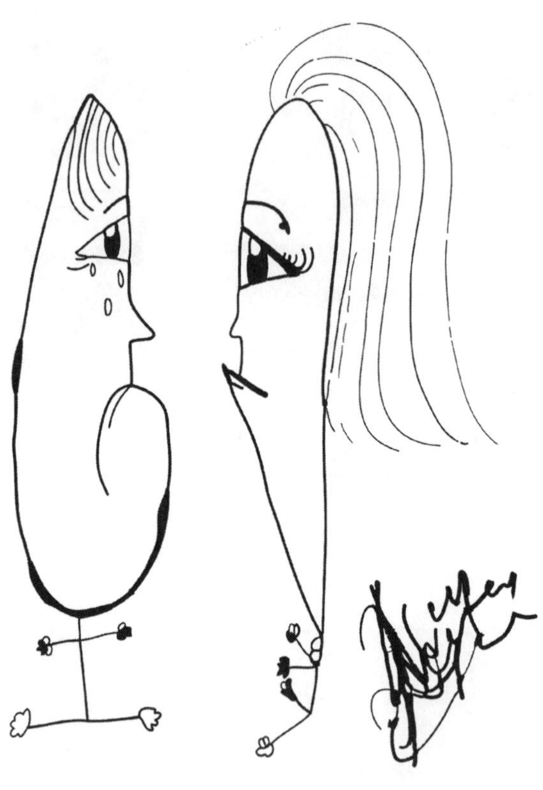

Rambling Dan

Oh my god,
Is there a god?
Is there a higher being?
Are there gates,
Of pearly white?
Or are we just believing?
Before now,
I've sat in sought,
And in searching for meaning,
I've fought for thought.

You fucked up in 1989

It started with a pony ride,
From then I can taste apple cider,
A pumpkin patch and shot gun by pilots side,
Air shows, push ups with marines,
Stuffed animals, and plastic sales pitches,
A garage band as a yard sale sign,
Goldfish zoom,
One by one, by two,
I swam a lake, city at bottom,
A boat at wake,
A family still docked,
Birthdays split in two,
Santa came twice,
Now he won't come at all,
The chimney sweep has lost it's charm,
Ring-a-round-a-rosie,
The dozens always die,
Odor of dead fish,
We threw the curtains back,
I didn't wave goodbye,
The pilot let me take control,
Only chance I'd ever be free,

Life's unanswered questions always on my mind,

If only it stopped at ten.

Once on Broadway

It's a needle on a record,

A hand on a clock,

Weighing me down,

Scales the proof,

I'm no expert in perfect posture,

Another correction in need of correcting,

I'm not perfect, and hard to believe . . . Neither are you,

Wake up sleeping beauty,

I don't want the honors,

There's something you can't do???

Applause, applause,

The great sir couldn't cure himself.

Born

The city has chased me away,
From its blinding lights to fear the unknown,
Where was I born and raised?
In a shadow,
Daddy why'd you leave?
I know she's a lot to handle,
But 17 years have done one right,
I've learned to deal with those teeth,
Mommy taught my measurements by bottles,
And she fed her belly to calm her monsters,
Where are two years?
Sucked up in the clouds,
Let's sip some cider and take to the city,
The highway ahead is endless in sight,
Thankfully time has clung to my good side tonight.

Metro a go go

Take me back to snowy metro rides,
Long distance phone calls to the city,
Sleepy Saturdays spent sleeping in,
And coffee drinks for downtown,
Right hand, left hand,
Hand in hand, don't hand me off,
Take my lines and twist them to hurt me,
Didn't mean to say it,
Let's just go back to smiles and sex,
It's how we started anyway.

Sketches

There's this pain in my chest,
And fear in my mind,
This hole in my stomach is one of a kind,
My medication keeps me up all night,
Two bucks, and I'll be alright,
Call it pathetic, but I'm fine . . . Really,
Forget me, it'd be best that way,
I've walked a million steps,
But every step was a march,
I'm side to side inside,
And I'm perfectly fine . . . Really.

Bait and wait

You,

You are the worm in the apple of my eye,

And he,

He was the one to bring me back to life,

Forgetful friend of mine,

Forget me,

I play hard to get far too well,

And luck is a hand I dare gamble,

For every penny I've found on heads,

Ends up in a jar of misfortunes,

I'm ready to release you fish,

Back into the sea you go,

The water stabbed at your gills,

But you'll be fine, you're alive,

There's plenty more fish in the sea they say,

But I've been fishing all month, every god damn day.

Pause, rewind, mute

I'll reel you in,

Throw you back,

Sit, smoke, repeat,

Repetition and routine consume these bones,

Make me into something worthwhile,

It's completely impossible if you can't love yourself,

Who else will?

They don't care to,

What a cunt, what a crutch, you unlucky fuck,

Wondering the contents of a bag of bones,

Outcast and unaclaimed.

Holy

He said trust me,
So I said okay,
And I walked with him,
Followed him up a hill,
My God it was beautiful,
We drank,
We sang,
We laughed,
And my god it was beautiful,
He took my hand and we jumped.

Private Screening

You say stay,

Diagnosed with an uncureable cancer,

You say "But baby, you're the girl of my dreams."

That's funny, because you haven't slept in months,

On and on for trial and tribulation,

Jurors always resort to guilty,

And yet I stay, last of the pack,

"One more song, please just stay."

So I stayed, I woke in a hospital bed,

Nurses moving mouths in rhythm,

Pulse 62, skin pasty as glue,

It's a pity the last words were lies, so stay,

I did, gone now, gone for good,

I saw some writing scribbled with pen,

"Diagnosis . . . uncureable cancer?"

Again you win.

New years resolution

Another box of nails to swallow,
Well, sorry dear, but my throat is sore,
And my teeth are decaying like days,
From purging laughs and smiles,
Does it even matter?
You said you'd help if you could,
You're just feeding more lies,
I'll just go throw up again,
You've got to let me go now,
I can't hold this string any longer with sand paper fingers.

A thought

"Epic Tragedy," self explanatory,
The monster broke from chains,
Swinging them around, he's become dangerous,
Frankenstein is laughing and smiling,
As the Mona Lisa dies.

Free Trade

We stare through the stain glass windows,
So tragic and serene,
Your face on a crayon portrait,
On a tarnished guilt easel,
I stand alone,
A graffitied wall,
Fucked up and a static forecast,
My alliance with the angels,
Is nothing short of jealousy,
They lynched my love,
I saw it hanging from the tree,
Utopia is a back stabbing bitch,
A broken society left to reconstruct,
Yesterday is over,
Today is shit,
And tomorrow is mocking me,
From those hideous stain glass windows.

Red Leather Jacket

He crashed his car under the wishing bridge,
Her heart fell heavy with woes and sighs,
Flashing lights,
City sounds,
The rain is now pouring all around,
Cats and dogs, now face down,
When you go to shake my hand,
I scratch my nails across your skin,
Glass left for breaking,
Love left for making,
A smoking car,
A fire's flame,
The world consumed,
In a loosing game,
The light won't bend in a hollow room,
So I let myself break and bruise,
As we slept away the Monday blues,
Tripping off fragments of love,
Splintered off the giant oak,
The man struck under the wishing bridge,
A wish is wasteful,
A cry is expensive,

All that's left is an empty wallet now,
And embedded in the burning car,
A photo id.

Freezing in the garage

She comes home and yells,
As we all fall apart,
The hatred in the walls,
The bleeding of our hearts,
These walls are screaming,
Pain is permanent feeling,
I dreamt of your anger,
As it gets thrown in my face,
I wish I could tell you,
How we all hate it here,
How much we're all hurting,
Hateful thoughts leave you alone,
Greedy for more,
But it was right in front of you,
Sitting on the table,
Ready for you to reach,
For seconds,
Minutes are consuming,
An hour is far too long,
To hear your apology,
Would be an epic eulogy,
Kind and perfect in every way,

But another thing promised,

Those are words you will never say.

Little Dreamer

Dancing on clouds, walking on the moon,
These are things I dream in my room,
Sitting on my bed when homework is done,
Dreaming of a land with bunches of fun,
Lollipops and gumdrops surrounding my head,
All I want to do is go back to bed,
So I tried and tried to lull myself to sleep,
but when I closed my eyes I heard a "creeeeeak."
I sat straight up with my eyes big and wide,
I knew I wasn't alone, so I tried to hide,
But when I pulled the blankets over my face,
I peeked through the covers and saw outer space!
Wow! There's another shooting star,
And look! There's an alien driving a car,
Then I looked to my left and saw a black hole,
So I kicked a soccer ball in and screamed "GOOOOOAL!"
"Goal?" I thought to myself,
There are no soccer balls in outer space,
Next thing I knew I was on a foot chase,
"Find the guy!", "Hey check in here!"
I saw a man running white with fear,
"Come over here!" I yelled to the man,
"Hey, over here . . . there's a garbage can."

I shoved him in and took off hopping,
Got caught up in a group that was be-bopping,
I joined in to hear all the fun,
but just as I did, out came the sun,
"The sun . . . already!". . . I don't want to go to school,
Mr. T came up behind me . . . "I pity you fool."
When I was walking the stairs up to my house,
I came across a bluegrass mouse,
Oh no way . . . now I know I am asleep,
I pinched my check and my alarm clock beeped,
I WAS DREAMING, I'M STILL IN BED!!!,
When I laid down, I must of just hit my head,
Wow, that was such an amazing dream,
I even got to play for a soccer team,
It felt so real, my team got creamed,
And all this happened just as I dreamed.

Recliner Chair

He holds the gun to her head,
His voice cracks,
She sheds a tear,
A tear of joy, but a tear of pain,
She can't remember the last time,
The last time she was able to smile,
His palms are sweating now,
She closes her eyes,
His pulse becomes rapid,
As does hers,
His eyes grow wide,
Hers shrink and retract,
Her body is trembling,
His hands start to shake,
She can't even swallow,
He can't even breathe,
He says "I . . . I'm sorry,"
She opened her eyes,
He moves to the chair where she sits,
She lets out a sigh and a smile,
He regains his breath,
His finger slipped,
She fell asleep in his favorite chair.

Wine Glass

I don't wish on stars any more,
They burn and fall too hard,
Always losing hope,
When they end up in my yard,
What's the point in wishing,
When they never come true,
Wasting your breath on words,
And actions you'll never do,
The bullets shine like candles,
The cake is fully loaded,
I'll take a million pills,
Each one sugar coated,
This bittersweet suicide is all I need to survive,
Watching the days fill this fucking calendar,
Cross them out with a permanent marker,
I can't hold this smile for much longer,
Losing a second of your time,
I'll sit alone and drink my wine.

When I got misplaced

You threw me away like an old pair of shoes,
And changed the channel like some bad news,
Drown me quickly, I don't want to see,
Don't think I can handle what happened to me,
Open my book,
Find your favorite line,
Re-read,
Repeat,
Retire your tired eyes,
And the questions so long, always unanswered,
And the answers so short, and unfaithful,
Cut along my ribs, and pull out my heart,
Spit shine it up and throw it in your pocket,
Cut along my jaw line and rip off my face,
Crop and paste to fit your locket.

It's not me, it's you

It's not that I want to die,

I just don't want to live,

I take what I'm given,

But what is it I give?

I give my time,

I give my smile,

I give a dime or two,

But it's never worth while,

You say "you're no good",

You say "just give up",

What you said hurts,

I'm gonna go throw up now,

You want to help,

You want to save me,

Maybe you should realize,

I need you to leave me alone,

Shut up, walk away, let me die,

Come to the funeral,

Wear a tie and suit,

Shed a smile, but please don't you cry.

T-9 Rhyme

If only,

I awake,

I stay lonely,

Likely to break,

Remember these eyes,

Don't count time,

Multiplying lies,

Sex became crime,

Your countless

Calculator . . . divide . . .

Clear it all.

Adopting the Ocean

The sky was a month late,
We all knew her fate,
Sitting alone, we wait,
Until the new due date,
She gave birth to a boy,
Left him on the road,
He did not bring joy,
She lightened up her load,
The ocean sunk in his eyes,
His skin was soft and fair,
No one heard his cries,
The night she left him there,
She gave him no name,
She didn't give him love,
His hopeful return never came,
Shifted lanes, went back above,
He waited and he waited,
But she never did come,
Got himself frustrated,
Burnt out by sun,
His life was taken,

This surprised even me,
How he struggled for the light,
We lost our eyes of deepest seas,
They pray for his tiny soul,
Gather by candlelight and weep,
Resting now, chilling hole,
For the son she didn't keep . . .
We love you.

No longer,
Do I belong here

Shoot the messenger bag,
Spill all it contains,
Keep pace, don't lag,
Bring me the remains,
Of a city torn by hail,
The burnt bridges at wake,
A great beginning, great fail,
Adding to the list yet another mistake,
Pulling the load uphill,
A mudslide to follow,
Losing all your will,
And pride to swallow,
Choking on lies told,
Coughing up tears,
Buy back what was sold,
Wrapped up in the years,
Battle what once was,
Charmed by a smile,
Do it, just cause',
Wrapping control in denial,
Stand up for what you own,

Not much but a name,

To all the patches you've sewn,

Circumnavigate,

All in all,

Losing this game.

Teatime at half past the moon

When I was a kid,
I prayed every night,
When I was a kid,
I slept with a night light,
When I was a kid,
I played hopscotch,
Now, I drink it,
When I was a kid,
I skipped some stones,
When I was a kid,
Never broke momma's bones,
When I was a kid,
I thought dreams came true,
Truly that's amusing,
When I was a kid,
I cried when I fell,
When I was a kid,
I was terrified of hell,
Forgive and forget,
Look back and regret,
Things I should have done,

Fights I should have won,
Words I should have said,
I'd never get outta bed,
Now that I'm older,
My blood flows colder,
I don't cry when I fall,
I cry when I hit a wall,
Forget the past,
Doesn't matter what we did,
Nothing ever lasts,
And I'm still just a kid.

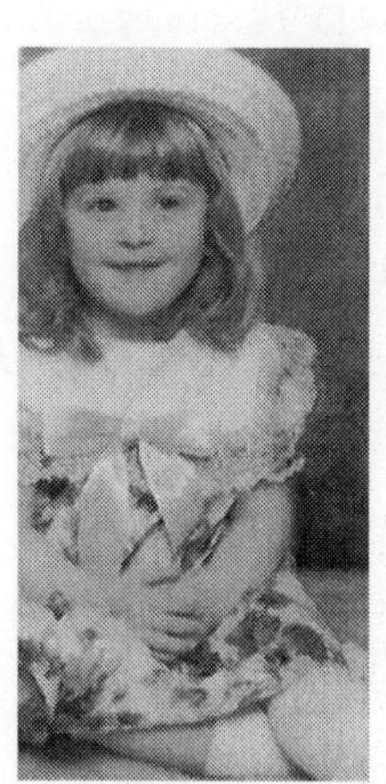

To PoPs:

THANKS SO MUCH FOR SHOWING INTEREST IN MY BOOK! IT MEANS ALOT. PLEASE ENJOY!! SPREAD THE WORD. :) ESPECIALLY IF YOU KNOW SOMEONE FALLING INTO A DEPRESSION. NO ONE EVER HAS TO FEEL ALONE.

[signature]

Author photo by Vincenzo Frattarola

Simone Le Ann has a heart of gold in a silver market. She is from another time and place where honor and courage were valued. Simone is compassionate to a flaw.

Simone takes tiny snapshots of life and paints them into elegant poetic metaphors. She writes from a place we've all been, and recites thoughts we all wish we'd said aloud. She is the answer to the question young adults have been asking for years.

Follow her on twitter at: www.twitter.com/LittleRabb1t

Made in the USA
Charleston, SC
10 January 2012